New
design in
Sweden

↓ *Stockholm New* publicizes the best Sweden has to offer in design and photography.

→ Brighten your everyday routine with Nina Job's bags for Design House Stockholm.

For most of the 1990s Swedish design has been in the international spotlight, and today it is more vital, energetic, diverse and innovative than ever. International design awards are pouring in, networks have been developed, and as a result more and more Swedish designers are now working with clients in every corner of the world. There have never been so many applicants for programmes of education in design, Swedish politicians and embassies are showing intense interest in design, and manufacturing industry has finally woken up to the fact that design is a crucial factor in competition, largely due to the battle of the mobile phones being waged between Swedish Ericsson and Finnish Nokia, which has now become a matter of pure design. Design has finally taken the step from the arts pages over to the business sections, and the attention and plaudits certainly seem to have given a great boost to the self-confidence of both designers and manufacturers.

What has really been going on, how do things look today, and what can we say about the future of Swedish design? How can we define what is typically Swedish, and who and what are the designers, manufacturers, products and qualities that arouse such curiosity and enthusiasm for Swedish design wherever it makes its appearance?

The aim of this brochure is to provide an overview of the contemporary Swedish design scene with the focus on industrial design. A scene characterized by heritage and tradition, but also by powerful new development thanks to increased internationalization and the revolt of the younger generation, particularly in the crafts field, against the kind of Swedishness that has been in focus for so long and won so many international awards. For it cannot be denied that the classical style labels of the last century, "Swedish Grace" and "Swedish Modern", are still very viable and attractive, especially in consumer goods, even if we tend to

↑ Mårten Claesson, Eero Koivisto and Ola Rune designed the Pebbles seat for Italian Cappellini.

use colour a lot more now than we used to. If you combine these external features with the venerable sincerity of the Made in Sweden brand as a warranty for functionality, ergonomics and attention to the needs of the user, then you get what still characterizes cutting-edge Swedish design, the development and renewal of unique Swedish qualities.

SPREADING THE IMAGE

The international interest in Swedish design today was sparked off in the early 1990s by a handfull of energetic missionaries using the name Swecode (Swedish Contemporary Design). This was a collaboration between the young manufacturers Asplund,

"honest and user-friendly"

→ Corona, a Rörstrand china service by Jonas Bohlin.

Box Design, cbi, David design and Forminord with the ambition of creating a space for Swedish design to express itself and show what it was capable of at international level. A forum expressly created to bring out the best in furniture, home furnishings and lighting. Their activities were well-timed, since both postmodernism and the overheated economy had just collapsed, which led to the basic Swedish ideals giving an answer to the question about what would follow the excesses of style and material of the 1980s. Our traditional designs offered the honesty, frugality and user-friendliness that were now in demand. This was combined with a credibility based on democratic ideas concerning gender equality, ecology and solidarity in Swedish society. In the words of Italian designer Vico Magistretti, Swedes have never used any particular style, but have always rooted their work in something deeper and more genuine.

The Swedish and the international press in general, and the British and Swedish magazines Wallpaper and Stockholm New in particular, leapt aboard the bandwagon and started wheels rolling in other media too, at international furniture fairs and gradually in Swedish manufacturing industry. The attraction was first and foremost in the design, of course, but also in the modern Swedish attitude which was described as socially aware,

↓ Yalla! yoghurt bottle. ("Yalla!" means "come on!" in several immigrant languages and is a popular expression among urban youngsters.) Designers: Lowe Brindfors and Mitte Blomqvist.

The style labels Swedish Grace and Swedish Modern were coined in the 1920s and 30s by foreign journalists to describe as typically Swedish a sense of blond ease, elegance, and lightness and sparse decoration. These epithets also characterized the objects exhibited at the big household goods exhibition H55 held in Helsingborg in 1955, which summed up the ideas of five decades concerning a modern and improved lifestyle and marked a high point of the Swedish Modern style in the last century.

↓ Jeans pelt; Emma Linde's degree project at HDK Textile Art 2002.

equitable, relaxed and creative in relation to the highly traditional furniture industry. Swedish design was often marketed together with other Swedish forms of expression like music, fashion and food.

When it was obvious that the new style was a success, Swedish politicians woke up and realized that design and other forms of creative industry were a first-class tool for marketing Sweden as a vital, international, modern society. In brief, it was a question of rebranding Sweden, moving from the qualitative, secure and slightly boring Volvo ideal to an image of a bolder and more creative nation. The ever-alert Minister for Industry, Employment and Communications Leif Pagrotsky decided to use Swedish music, design, fashion, IT know-how and food in establishing a new image of contemporary Sweden.

In the wake of this drive, many productive political and private sector creative initiatives have been launched, and as a result many Swedes today move naturally from one international client to another. Here are some examples: the architectural firm of Claesson Koivisto Rune has designed a cultural centre in Kyoto, while their colleague Thomas Sandell has been cooperating with one of the biggest construction companies in the world, Mori Building Corporation. The illustrious furniture company Gärsnäs furnished three rooms in the new Library of Alexandria (designed by Norway's Snøhetta) while newer companies Offecct and Swedese were given loud ovations at the most recent furniture fair in Milan. The Swedish rock-pianist Robert Wells played for an audience of at least a thousand million people when he outclassed both Britney Spears and Enrique Iglesias as the only western artists appearing on a TV-hosted environmental gala in China. The Swedish band, the Hives, is said to be one of the most popular in Britain, and interest in things Swedish has spread to our fashion with such representa-

↓ Award-winning dumper trucks, developed by Nya Perspektiv Design in close cooperation with Volvo Construction Equipment. Security, comfort and an enhanced driving experience.

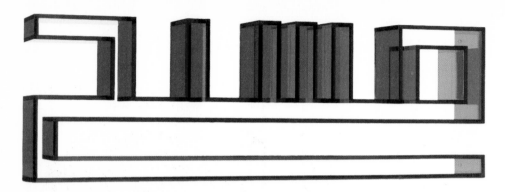

tives as Tiger, J. Lindeberg and Whyred. Star chefs like Karl Ljung, Henrik Håkansson and Andreas Hedlund are highly sought after as are many Swedish illustrators and graphic designers like Joel Berg and Lotta Kühlhorn, who are often engaged by foreign magazines. Sought after by art galleries, too, as witness Henrik Nygren and Greger Ulf Nilsson's identity profile for Baltic in Newcastle. Stockholm Design Lab has made waves for Swedish graphic design in the air, both via the new profile for the airline SAS and the design of the most modern final yet of the Eurovision Song Contest, held in Stockholm in the year 2000, with stage settings by Mikael Varhelyi and more than 100 million viewers around the world.

These designers and many others are today spreading the new Swedishness throughout the world. Not too bad for a country of around nine million inhabitants, previously known mainly for Abba, Ikea, Volvo, Saab and one or two Wimbledon champions!

MODERNITY AND DEMOCRACY

"One really positive thing is that modern Swedish design plays a clear role in everyday life, it's there, it's accepted. Go to other countries where modern design is for a certain elite. Where only a minority is aware of it. In Sweden you arrive at the airport, you see the cars, you go to restaurants, see how people dress, the mobile telephones etc. Everything shows how modern your environment and whole country is."

These are the words of German designer Konstantin Grcic in a conversation with his Swedish colleague Björn Dahlström about nationality and attitudes to design. Of course, it might not be so very difficult to be modern in a small country where most people like to furnish their homes with Ikea's products, wear

H&M fashions or drive Volvos and Saabs – all extremely design-conscious companies. Through the centuries, Swedes have been inspired by foreign fashions in style, and have used them in conjunction with our simple methods of production and "impoverished" materials to create our own simplified, spare and undecorated version of – a Swedish style. Light natural materials have contributed to the blond impression, as has inspiration from the countryside and the Swedish light, which is softer than in countries where the sun climbs higher into the sky. Today this pure, light simplicity we know as Swedish is not just produced by Swedes, but we have the greatest credibility thanks to our heritage.

Grcic captures the most essential characteristics of Swedish design, and perhaps its greatest claim to uniqueness. It is democratic, intended to benefit everybody. This is seen in the care shown to vulnerable groups in society, such as the disabled, in the design of public premises and a striving to achieve ergonomically optimized working conditions.

The furniture company Ikea has explained the concept of democratic design in the following way: "If you grow up in Sweden you will know – either from your father or from society in general – that those who are a little worse off ought to have the same opportunities as those who are a little better off." The company today stands as the greatest disseminator of Swedish design with 172 large-scale stores in 37 countries. So when it comes to democratic accessibility, both financial and geographical, they are in a class of their own. In an encouraging move, Ikea has recently been putting more emphasis on its own design and less on imitation, and this also goes for H&M, Ikea's counterpart in the field of Swedish fashion.

Volvo's former head of design, Peter Horbury, recently explained democracy in design by saying that "Swedish design

"a multi-cultural society"

↑ Rodrigo Gutierrez' degree project at Beckman's School of Design in 2001, a series of "Sweden" stamps reflecting a multi-cultural society.

→ Welder's helmet and Adflo breathing mask designed by Ergonomidesign.

mirrors a caring society". This caring is deeply rooted in Swedish politics, too, where various public ombudsmen watch vigilantly over the rights of individuals and minorities. They include the Disability Ombudsman, the Equal Opportunities Ombudsman, the Ombudsman against Discrimination on the grounds of Sexual Orientation and the Ombudsman against Ethnic Discrimination.

LOBBYING AND IMPROVING SOCIETY

Design has long been important in relation to both the improvement of Swedish society and a Swedish sense of identity. A desire for good design to be accessible to the masses has been voiced by both politicians and lobbyists, both as individuals and by way of the Swedish Society of Crafts and Design, which was founded in 1845. Three of the most influential propaganda writings to characterize the last century in this respect were Skönhet för alla (Beauty for all), Vackrare vardagsvara (More

Beauty for all was written in 1899 by polemicist and author Ellen Key, who considered that light, natural and white-scrubbed surfaces generated a beauty that was ennobling for humanity. More beautiful things for the home was published in 1919 by Svenska Slöjdföreningen (the then Swedish Society of Crafts and Design) and written by the art historian Gregor Paulsson, who emphasized the importance of cooperation between industry and artists to ensure the esthetic appeal of the outcome. Accept, written after the Stockholm exhibition of 1930, and whose authors included Gregor Paulsson and the architects Gunnar Asplund and Sven Markelius, sang the praises of industrialism and the new functional architecture of the new age, and had the ambition of explaining, influencing and winning broad acceptance for the ongoing changes in society and thus a belief in the opportunities of the new epoch – and its architecture.

→ Camilla Diedrich's bubble lamp BPL for Annell Ljus + Form.

beautiful things for the home), and Acceptera (Accept). The last of these, ideologically a manifesto for functionalism, went hand in hand with the ideas of the Social Democratic Prime Minister of the 1930s, Per Albin Hansson, who thought that both the expression and the social awareness of functionalist architecture suited his vision of the Swedish welfare state down to the ground.

Today the foremost lobbyists for good design in relation to politicians, service providers, manufacturers and private individu-

← Anna von Schewen's kitchen at housing expo Bo01 in Malmö; welcoming, functional and flexible.

→ Reclining chair with built-in sleeping bag; Björn Dahlström's Relax for cbi.

↓ Thomas Eriksson's E-Seat
for Offecct.

↓ Gustaf Nordenskiöld's knife
and spoon express our need for
comprehensibility and roots.

→ Satellite link IPT Suitcase – a
portable satellite link for TV and web
broadcasts, perfect for journalists in
inaccessible locations. By Reload
Design for Swedish Satellite Systems.
Designers: Tor Bonnier and Lars Hofsjö.

SWE DISH

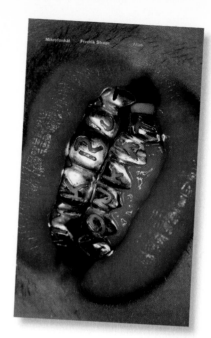

↑ Book cover for *Mikrofånkåt*, graphic design by Karl Grandin.

als are Svensk Form (the Swedish Society of Crafts and Design) and Svid (the Swedish Industrial Design Foundation). The Swedish Society of Crafts and Design has been commissioned by the government to promote high-quality Swedish design both at home and abroad. This is done by way of exhibitions, publications like the periodical Form Designtidskriften (in both Swedish and English), and awards like those for Excellence in Swedish Design, Select Design and Young Swedish Design, which are intended to encourage exemplary design and to remind the general public that design affects every product field.

The Swedish Industrial Design Foundation has been commissioned by the Ministry of Industry, Employment and Communications to encourage Swedish industry to use design as a means of competition and to improve awareness of the importance of design. The ambition is to get companies to prioritize design, to broaden the concept of design to all levels of society and to make Sweden a world leader in the field.

↓ Cosmos by Gunilla Allard for Lammhults: winner of awards like the Blueprint/100% Design Award 2002.

POLITICAL AWARENESS

A lot is still being done today. There are a great number of central government, regional and municipal design initiatives, all aimed at raising awareness of the advantages of high-quality design for both industrial competition and the quality of life of the everyday consumer. And naturally to generate growth and give Sweden a chance of climbing back up from its current ranking of 17 in the prosperity and welfare league tables. Twenty years ago Sweden was number 4!

To give a few examples – in 1998, the Swedish parliament adopted the architectural policy plan "Future design – an action programme for architecture and design", in order to emphasize the importance of investing in high quality housing and public

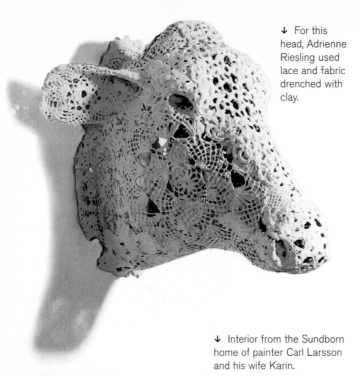

↓ For this head, Adrienne Riesling used lace and fabric drenched with clay.

↓ Interior from the Sundborn home of painter Carl Larsson and his wife Karin.

The nationally revered painter Carl Larsson and his wife Karin established the trend for light, airy and refined simplicity in interior decoration with their own home towards the end of the 19th century. Publicists of the day warned Swedish housewives against brightly coloured wallpaper, "as this gives the room a vulgar appearance", and in the 1940s the Swedish Society of Crafts and Design gave courses in home-making in which they taught people how to avoid the ugliness of kitsch.

areas in combination with careful management of both financial and ecological resources.

In the same year, the Swedish Ministry for Foreign Affairs had the courage to ask the young trio of architects Claesson Koivisto Rune to decorate the ambassadorial residence in Berlin. This was at a moment when all the Nordic embassies were newly built, the Swedish one having been designed by Wingårdh Arkitekter. In order to make an affectionate gesture of solidarity with their contemporary Swedish colleagues, they furnished the residence with the best of new Swedish furniture, textiles, carpets and objets d'art. And as a result all the other ambassadors are said to be thoroughly envious of their Swedish colleague!

In 1998, the Ministry of Industry, Employment and Communications played a leading role in funding a pilot project called EkoDesign which was intended to encourage designers to produce new, environmentally friendly products. The adviser to the project, Dutch industrial designer Geert Timmers, thinks that Sweden is among the best in the world at environmentally aware product development.

Sweden's largest union organisation, the Swedish Trade Union Confederation (LO), took a responsible step in the year 2000 and published the book "Sweden in good shape" with the objective of obtaining competence development for industrial workers in the design field, thus improving both their workplaces and increase the number of job opportunities.

The Minister for Culture proclaimed 2001 as Architecture Year, and in the run-up to Sweden's Presidency of the EU in the same year, great efforts were put into giving the public meeting venues a contemporary Swedish flavour. The government commissioned architects Thomas Sandell and Gert Wingårdh to decorate the venues with the best that Sweden had to offer.

At the time of writing, there is talk of proclaiming 2005 as the

Year of Design, at the same time as a proposal for a new national programme for design as a force for development in the private and public sectors, to be called "Sweden Innovative Caring Society", is awaiting a final decision.

Important efforts are also being made by the Swedish Institute and Swedish embassies and consulates around the world, often in cooperation with the Swedish Society of Crafts and Design, which have further heightened interest in Swedish design by way of exhibitions, seminars and study trips for journalists. A good example is the exhibition Swedish Style in Tokyo which was put on for the third occasion in October 2002.

STRATEGIC DESIGN – A SWEDISH STRENGTH

There are a lot more voices in the chorus heightening awareness about the positive role of design in industry, however. In recent years successful companies in strategic design and architecture have been set up and in this way helped to deepen understanding in industry of the effect design can have in relation to products, the environment and communications. In fact, Sweden has become a successful nation in this field, and firms like Ytterborn & Fuentes, SandellSandberg, Stockholm Design Lab, Bas Retail, Koncept and Strategisk Arkitektur provide examples of pioneers deepening the knowledge of both Swedish and foreign clients about corporate design. What is design, what should it be used for and how, what is to be given shape and who is most suitable for doing this?

A closely studied project, and Sweden's most comprehensive design commission ever, is Stockholm Design Lab's new profile for SAS. A project called SAS 2000+, which was presented in 1998 and which permeates everything from aircraft and airport lounges to customer information, salt sachets, ticket handling

↓ Thomas Sandell.

→ Innovative thinking in child safety: lifejacket by Caran Design for Neil Pryde Ltd.

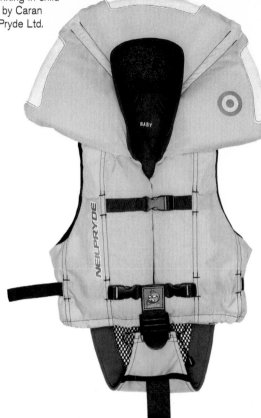

↑ Gunnar Leijonberg designed Husqvarna's battery-driven, self-charging lawnmower. You relax in the sun while the Auto Mower does the work.

← BabyBjörn's child's plate and spoon won the Excellent Swedish Design award in 2001.

↓ Rather more off-beat examples of Swedish rooms are provided by Umbilical Design's interiors for extreme environments like oil rigs, space capsules, submarines and polar research stations.

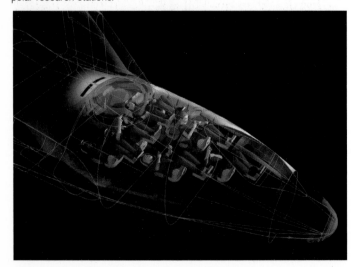

↓ Volvo xc90, described by Peter Horbury as "masculine, but not macho; muscular, but not aggressive".

and staff uniforms. The work has involved going through the approximately 2,000 different articles encountered by a passenger in the form of communications, services, products, etc, and adding to them the ideas, content and appearance of the new strategy. SAS's own motto, and a good summary of the result is: "It's Scandinavian."

HEALTHY SCEPTICISM

If you ask glass artist and designer Ulrica Hydman-Vallien, colourful in both her personality and her artistic expression and the best-selling Swedish designer both at home and abroad, about Swedishness, she will tell you there is no such thing as a Swedish trait, only individual ones. And there is of course a certain amount of truth in this! To claim that all Swedish design is fastidiously blond is about as true as saying that all Swedes are fair-haired and all Italian design is synonymous with Cappellini. Critical voices in the field of contemporary Swedish design think that the traditional notion of Swedish design is not easy to develop or to renew. This is partly because award-winning products, such as those receiving the Excellent Swedish Design accolade and getting shown off in the media and on the international scene, with few exceptions conform to the traditional epithets of blond, cool and unornamented.

Those who are most critical and open to development are the younger generation of Swedish craftsmen, who comment more freely on their day and age by questioning the norms, limits and aesthetics of the field and the materials at their disposal. A questioning of the conformist establishment such as most recently occurred in Sweden in the 1960s, and which led to a renewal and development of "Swedishness" in the art industry, too. In the contemporary resistance we can see relatively recent

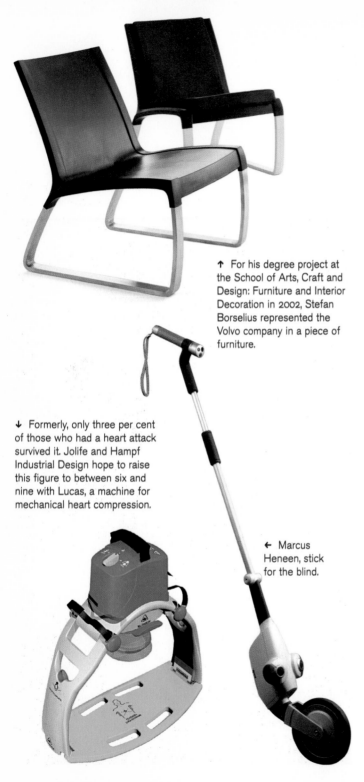

↑ For his degree project at the School of Arts, Craft and Design: Furniture and Interior Decoration in 2002, Stefan Borselius represented the Volvo company in a piece of furniture.

↓ Formerly, only three per cent of those who had a heart attack survived it. Jolife and Hampf Industrial Design hope to raise this figure to between six and nine with Lucas, a machine for mechanical heart compression.

← Marcus Heneen, stick for the blind.

names at work, led by individuals like Zandra Ahl, Gustav Nordenskiöld, Frida Fjellman, Hanna Ljungström, Andrea Djerf and Jakob Robertsson. In their world, jeans candlesticks are draped with pearl necklaces, and glass vases wear belts. Teeth and firewood inspire potters to new shapes, a pig's snout in glass becomes a lamp, cheap and costly materials are mixed irreverently and the content is often more important than the finish. Pop culture is sampled in confectionery colours and ceramic polar bears engage in bloody battle.

Old norms and watchwords are turned upside-down, and if the Swedish media kept a better eye on this developing craftsmanship, then the publicity and discussion created would hasten more dynamic developments. If these forms of expression are also spread internationally, then a broader and deeper dimension of Swedish design identity will be communicated.

THE SWEDES IN A NUTSHELL

This kind of expression is slowly but surely helping to soften up ingrained Swedish rigidity. The British designer James Irvine has said that "modern Swedish design looks the way it does because of the stiffness of Swedish thinking. It has none of the creative chaos you find in Italian heads".

To get an even better grasp of Swedish design it might help to give a very sweeping and general description of our most salient characteristics: the Swedes are said to be open, friendly, and inquisitive, but a bit shy and stiff, too. Some people think they are as square-cut and rigid as the Germans, melancholic and trapped in the vice-like grip of "Jante's Law", a who-do-you-think-you-are syndrome often manifested in the humiliation of those who are enjoying success. Swedes are widely-travelled and good at languages – they start learning English by the age of nine at the latest and often add another language later. They are reputed to be suckers for novelty, and fashions spread through the country like wildfire. Furthermore, they are almost embarrassingly conformist, don't like standing out, and hate being different. Swedes always choose flexibility and compliance rather than friction. They want the same car as their neighbour, but a bit nicer, just so long as nobody can see they've got money! They take a protective interest in their countryside and their summer cottages – a good 40 per cent of them have their own. Swedes love sports and active recreation, and take evening classes in everything from carpentry and pottery to photography and sewing. This is probably due to the self-sufficiency genes they have inherited from their small but independent farming ancestors. A good man can take care of himself! Furthermore, they usually vote Social Democrat and have been doing so for the better part of the past 70 years. To all this they can proudly add the assessments of Swedish designers made by international clients; "unassuming, cooperative, painstaking, modest, skilled communicators with an ear-to-the-ground awareness of international developments".

THE HUMAN ATTITUDE

Swedish industrial designers are said to be more interested in function than appearance, and to prefer to find new solutions to everyday problems rather than to sell tried and tested ideas in new and trendy packaging. This brings us to industrial design, a field in which for the most part the prefix Swedish has internationally come to be associated with ergonomic tools and assistive technology for the disabled. This last has been showcased as epoch-making by the Museum of Modern Art in New York, and Swedes have spread everything from bread-saws,

↓ A garment from the Boob breast-feeding collection. Designer: Mia Seipel.

← One of Per B. Sundberg's ceramic radios.

↓ Updated pioneering spirit in the Settler series by Thomas Sandell for Allinwood.

↓ Saab's latest pride and joy, the 9-3x, a "cross-over coupé" combining a sports car's image with four-wheel drive.

shower- and wheelchairs to pliers and children's cutlery throughout the world.

It was in the university-occupying 1960s that the working environment, conservation of resources and solidarity came into focus. A number of small-scale industrial design bureaus were set up, many of them still active, on the basis of what Americans call the human attitude. In their work the emphasis was on products that facilitated everyday life for the disabled and lightened work in heavy industry, as well as on ergonomics with the user in sharp focus. Concepts that are deeply rooted in today's Swedish industrial design, which at its best assumes the role of a social reformer with a desire to simplify and improve life for the consumer. Today Swedish industrial design is also strong in fields such as protective equipment, automotive design, children's products, ergonomic tools and medical apparatus.

A good example of the above is Atlas Copco's Cobra drill, developed by a team including industrial designer Björn Dahlström. It has an on-button and an off-button, it runs on unleaded petrol, reduces vibration so the user is saved considerable physical discomfort, and is all-in-all a masterpiece of user-friendly ergonomics. Thanks to these qualities it has been a sales hit around the world.

Further examples of award-winning and turnover-boosting products are Hörnell's Speedglas® 9000 welder's helmet, which was developed in cooperation with Ergonomidesign, and its recent add-on, the equally award-winning motorized breathing mask, Adflo, The design is characterized by good ergonomics, tough, robust lines and flexibility for the user which all helps to boost professional pride and improve the working environment. What made the Hörnell company discover the advantages of industrial design was a project initiated by the Swedish Industrial Design Foundation in cooperation with the municipality, which gave small and medium-sized companies the opportunity to work with an industrial designer while the municipality bore part of the cost. It was a very successful initiative!

But although manufacturers are very interested in design, ignorance is still rife. The designer's crucial role in industrial teamwork is still not clear to everybody, and the notion that "design just makes everything more expensive" is widespread – an assumption which must be confronted with the view of Volvo's former head of design that only 3–4 per cent of a product's development costs are design-related. An inspirational example of a company that changed its attitude is Conroy Medical, which doubled its turnover in a year thanks to its cooperation with Ergonomidesign. It did this with a welding gun for sealing blood tubes, a product on which very high demands are made. It needs to be easy to understand, safe and easy to use, portable, functional, attractive and ergonomically acceptable. Aspects such as recycling and environmental advantages also came into play in the production of HandySeal. The product turned out to be Conroy Medical's ticket to both the American and Japanese markets, and to top it all it won the Excellent Swedish Design award in 1999 and the prestigious German design award Roter Punkt 2002, which led to a series of articles in the international press.

A NEW, STRONG GENERATION

Today the industrial design companies Ergonomidesign, Zenit Design Group, No Picnic and Propeller are among the largest and most illustrious in the country. In the 1990s a new generation took over in the field, and the profession gained new status as industry realized that design could be an important tool in its competitive mix. Many of the companies launched at this time by

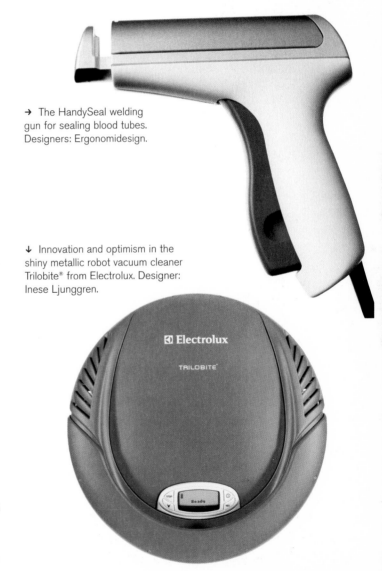

→ The HandySeal welding gun for sealing blood tubes. Designers: Ergonomidesign.

↓ Innovation and optimism in the shiny metallic robot vacuum cleaner Trilobite® from Electrolux. Designer: Inese Ljunggren.

↑ Award-winning Hug and Big Hug by Anna von Schewen for Gärsnäs.

↓ Part of Pia Wallén's collection for 2002.

newly-fledged industrial designers now have well-known clients and award-winning products to their name.

An example is No Picnic, founded in 1993, and now working for Ericsson, ABB, the European Space Agency and others. For the ESA they produced a refrigerator specially designed for space shuttles – the RFR, Refrigerator Freezer Rack, which makes it possible for astronauts to eat normal instead of freeze-dried food. The company has also been in the limelight for its armchair Lounger for Felicerossi in Italy, and for its Neonode mobile telephone for Sweden's youngest mobile phone company of the same name.

And the newly-fledged designers continue to impress. One example, winning the Young Swedish Design award, is Marcus Heneen's 2001 degree project at HDK, the University College of Design and Applied Arts and Crafts in Gothenburg. Spot is a wheeled stick for the blind, intended to guide and facilitate movement in urban environments for people with impaired vision, an electronic guide dog with built-in artificial intelligence and a GPS navigator, which when fully developed will be able to guide its user to any given address. Furthermore, the handle will be removable and capable of reading text using a built-in voice synthesizer. Let's keep our fingers crossed that these ambitions can be brought to fruition as the product is developed beyond its current prototype stage.

ATTRACTIVE PROGRAMMES OF EDUCATION

As far as design education is concerned, new programmes have been springing up like mushrooms since the mid-1990s, and the number of applicants has shot up in the past couple of years. The greatest attraction is exerted by programmes of education in industrial design, and many universities and colleges through-

out the country offer complete programmes or individual courses in the subject. The programmes meet high international standards and many of them offer broad, cross-disciplinary teaching spanning different fields of design, and form part of various international student exchange networks. The School of Arts, Craft and Design (Konstfack) and Beckman's School of Design in Stockholm, the School of Textiles in Borås, HDK (the University College of Design and Applied Arts and Crafts) in Gothenburg, the Lund Institute of Technology, and the College of Design at Umeå University are among the most popular.

The last of these has reason to be proud: it won the Swedish National Agency for Higher Education's nomination as the best college for future industrial designers, and an astounding 95 per cent of its students are headhunted by large companies both in Sweden and abroad (with which the college has close working relations) straight after taking their degrees. Umeå also has the country's most international orientation, with 30 per cent foreign students from 16 different countries in its Masters programmes and as many as 75 per cent in basic training. In addition, they have the only Masters programme in Transportation Design in the Nordic countries, besides programmes in Advanced Product Design and Interaction Design.

CARS, KIDS AND COUNTRYSIDE

An area in which Sweden has long been very strong is automotive design. Volvo and Saab are continuously developing security, comfort and performance by way of frequent minor innovations, all in an elegant and vigorous package. The latest addition to the star-studded firmament of Swedish automotive design is the Koenigsegg CC sports car, which has a very uncommon target group for a Swedish company; super-rich sports car collectors

"cars, kids and countryside…"

↓ Lotta Kühlhorn.

↓ Björn Dahlström's BDY for cbi.

around the world. There was a heated controversy following the Excellent Swedish Design award to Koenigsegg in 2001. Was this really socially improving, frugal, accessible design? Despite this, everyone agreed that the car was worth a prize for its looks.

Of course Swedish industrial design reflects other national ideals, too, like the desire to be close to nature and if possible in it, busy with outdoor activities. Recent examples of this are Björn Dahlström's white tent Camper, for the Fjällräven company, Gustav Nord's gracefully elegant ice-yacht Nord, and the children's life-jacket designed by Caran Design for Neil Pryde Ltd, which shows a remarkable degree of innovative thinking.

Talking of children, the BabyBjörn company has been creating products for more than forty years now, including its practical baby carrier, which has gladdened millions of parents and children around the world. In 2002, the company won the Roter Punkt award for its baby-friendly feeding spoon. The breast-feeding collection Boob is both child- and mother-friendly. Graphic designer Mia Seipel had the idea of a sweater with an overlap design that makes it easier for a baby to reach the breast while at the same time keeping it warm and protecting it from the gaze of curious strangers. Seipel took out a patent on her invention, and in 2000 she started the company Boob Design, whose fashion-conscious products have been a big hit with breast-feeding mothers in Scandinavia.

↓ Andrea Djerf's unusually shaped ceramic bowl.

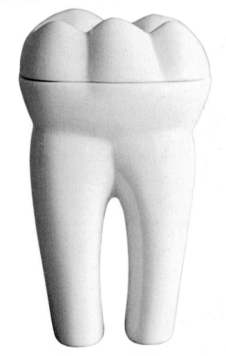

EVERYDAY QUALITY, FUNCTION, AND BEAUTY

Industrial design isn't the only field to have experienced a boom since a much-needed generational take-over – furniture, glass, ceramics and textiles have all benefited from youth and innovative thinking and a more outward-looking marketing approach.

After a dearth of big names, at least on the international

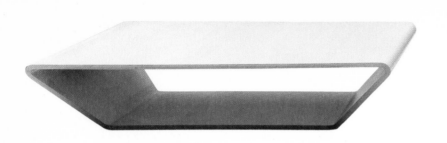

scene, a number of new stars were born in the 1990s in the generation which made its professional debut in the 1980s and the early 1990s. Architects and furniture designers like Thomas Sandell, Jonas Bohlin, Gunilla Allard, Mats Theselius, Jonas Lindvall, Anna von Schewen and the collaborative trio Mårten Claesson, Eero Koivisto and Ola Rune, to name but a few. Like Per B. Sundberg, Lena Bergström, Gunnel Sahlin and Ann Wåhlström in glass, ceramics virtuoso Pia Törnell, and Gunilla Lagerhem Ullberg and Pia Wallén in textiles. Not forgetting the astonishingly versatile industrial and graphic designer Björn Dahlström.

Their successes encouraged even more youngsters to go to design colleges and today yet another new and formidable wave of designers is beginning to make itself felt in the market. Some of the most influential of them are Monica Förster, Thomas Bernstrand, Anna Kraitz, Lars Pettersson, Helena Allard and Matti Klenell. These artisans are already leading developments in Swedish design, often in cooperation with companies that haven't seen innovation in a very long time.

SUCCESSES GALORE

The Swedish furniture scene is the largest and most active of the different consumer categories, and in recent years old-established companies, some of them nearing the century mark, have experienced a veritable boom thanks to their new tack of cooperating with young designers. Another reason for the improvement is that Stockholm International Furniture Fair has become an ever more significant trading venue, with a growing number of international exhibitors, visitors and journalists.

Many Swedish furniture companies, which have traditionally been oriented towards furnishing public premises, have adopted a new strategy and started to find their way into Swedish living-rooms. An example is Skandiform, which until the early 1970s was best known for its care sector furniture, but which has successfully broadened its range of products to include office and home furniture, using designers like Jonas Lindvall and Claesson Koivisto Rune. Gärsnäs, founded in 1893, has worked with Anna von Schewen, whose innovative experiments with curved solid wood furniture have taken the company's traditions into new areas.

Those companies which have hitherto been the most active at international level, such as Lammhults, Kinnarps, Källemo and Blå Station, now find themselves flanked by others thanks to domestic success stimulating first-time participation in furniture fairs in Cologne, New York and Milan, where recently such companies as Swedese and Offecct have made their debut and exhibited work created in cooperation between Swedish and foreign designers. Swedese works with craftsmen like Michael Young and James Irvine, while Offecct has used the skills of Karim Rashid, Marre Moerel, Jean-Marie Massaud, Alfredo Häberli and others. For Offecct, the successes it has enjoyed in the past two years have aroused an ambition to become one of Europe's most interesting design brands as quickly as possible, and if cited sales figures are to be believed, or the accolades of the international press, then they have every prospect of succeeding.

Last but not least, we should mention Snowcrash, a Swedish company born of a highly experimental Finnish furniture collection of the same name in 1997. Snowcrash works in a field bridging home and work, often with wholly innovative and very exciting products oozing function, creativity, playfulness and a high feel-good factor.

← Eero Koivisto and Ola Rune's Brasilia, a sculptural coffee table, compact and open volumes for Swedese.

←↓ Anki Gneib.

↓ Boxer, a chair with extensible foot and neck support, by Thomas Bernstrand for Söderbergs möbler.

↓ Erik Tidäng won the prestigious Bengt Julin scholarship in 2002.

← Part of Pia Wallén's collection for 2002.

↓ Anna Kraitz' self-assured lamp for Belysningsbolaget.

PROUD TRADITIONS

The most illustrious names in Swedish applied arts and crafts are the Orrefors and Kosta Boda glassworks and Rörstrand, the china manufacturers. Despite now having Danish and Finnish owners, respectively, these companies and brands are still deeply Swedish in spirit. These manufacturers also represent an important link in the chain between the uniqueness of art, the experimental craftsmanship possible with small product runs, and industrial mass production. Here too a large share of development takes place, both as regards technique and expression. For instance one of our virtuoso glass designers, Ingegerd Råman, has created successful hybrids in the form of hand-blasted but mass-produced glass.

Orrefors and Kosta Boda have been able to establish glass artists like Ulrica Hydman-Vallien, Kjell Engman and Bertil Vallien in the international market, and now it is the turn of a younger generation including Per B. Sundberg, Lena Bergström and Ann Wåhlström.

A generational shift is also under way in Svenska Glasbruk, an association of small- and medium-sized glassworks, where Anna von Schewen, Angelica Gustafsson, Carina Seth Andersson and Anki Gneib are contributing to a much-needed revitalization.

The flagship of Swedish craft manufacturing since 1726, Rörstrand China has followed some furniture companies in inviting foreign designers to work with it. It owes its most recent big successes to Pia Törnell and Jonas Bohlin, however, and the way they have developed products for the table that combine both beauty and function. Boda Nova and Höganäs Keramik are working successfully in the same field, producing glass, china and cutlery.

Like other industries, many textile companies have moved production abroad to meet competition from low-wage countries.

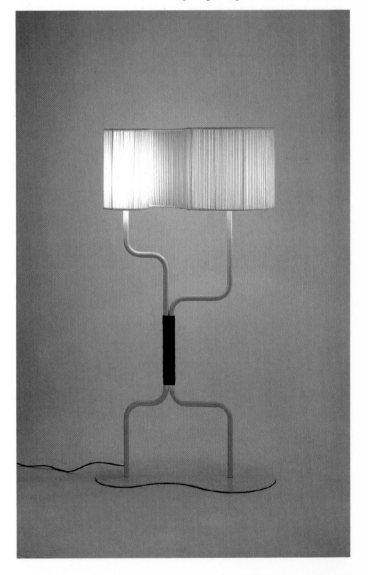

"Swedish fashion in the world"

An example of this is Linum, whose light checked and striped textiles have modernized a typical aspect of Swedish style, and whose production facilities are now located in India. Old companies like Ljungbergs and Almedahls combine classical 1950s patterns newly produced in Sweden with modern collections, while Klässbol remains Sweden's most important producer of linen goods.

Another venerable textile company is Kasthall, whose carpets testify to a rich tradition combined with constant innovative thinking. At the Milan furniture fair in 2001, some of the best-known Italian companies had adorned their booths with Gunilla Lagerhem Ullberg's most popular product, Moss, a deep-pile rug with glittering, incandescent shades of colour.

One of the smaller but most interesting textile companies is Saldo, which translates socially radical ideas and issues into textile patterns, the 1970s collective 10-Gruppen, and Designer's Eye, a family company whose various woollen felt products show off their highly innovative collaboration with designer Lena Bergström.

FASHION – SWEDISH SELLS

While on the subject of textiles, of course, Swedish fashion must not be left aside, even though it actually deserves a book to itself like our architecture and graphic design.

Swedish fashion is fresh, clean and cool, with a practical and simple foundation but plenty of urban and individual references. Like J. Lindeberg, Tiger and Filippa K, companies able to establish themselves in various parts of the world largely thanks to their Swedishness, joining H&M which reigns supreme in Swedish fashion with its more than 770 shops in 14 countries. The company's strength lies in its ability to rapidly turn broad

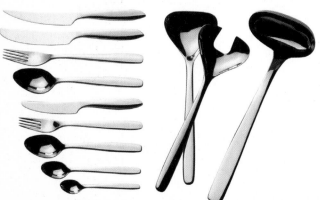

worldwide trends into clothes that most people can afford, combined with a selection of basic clothing essentials which have become the favourites of conscious consumers. A cheap H&M garment can be combined with a breathtakingly expensive one from the likes of American Bill Blass. And who should be head designer at Blass but the Swede Lars Nilsson, who has rapidly become the darling of American critics after having previously worked in Paris as Christian Lacroix's right-hand man.

The younger generation of Swedish designers and brands now leaving our shores includes names like Whyred, Lovisa Burfitt, Marina Kereklidou and Carin Rodebjer. At the Danish fashion fair CPH Vision, you can get the best annual overview of the actors in Swedish and Scandinavian fashion.

At the same time as Swedish fashion has grown stronger in recent years, Swedish fashion photography has been keeping up through its work for the world's best known fashion magazines.

AND NOW – APPLIED ARTS AND CRAFTS!

And the winner of the Dynamo scholarship for 2002 is – the craft gallery owner Inger Molin! "For deploying courage, tenacity and a unique sense of the exquisite to create what is currently the most interesting scene in that indeterminate area between art and the crafts."

The award of this prestigious scholarship to Stockholm-based Inger Molin by Sweden's Pictorial Artists' Fund can be seen as a rehabilitation for the arts and crafts after being overshadowed by industrial design during the 1990s. Swedish artisans have traditionally used state-subsidized cooperative institutions like Konsthantverkarna and Blås&knåda in Stockholm, and Lerverk and Sintra in Gothenburg as their window on the world. Since the turn of the millennium, however, the prestige and visibility of the

← Designer's Eye's felt hanging Cut by Lena Bergström.

←↓ JOL – Boda Nova's cutlery range by Jan Olsson Loftén.

↓ Ingegerd Råman.

field has been slowly but surely in the ascendant as the media and consumers tire of the repetitive character of industrial products and begin to appreciate the worth of the unique qualities offered by high-level craftsmanship. As the dynamic creative power of this field makes itself felt, people are beginning to say that the first decade of the 3rd millennium will belong to the crafts, after the reign of the fine arts in the 1980s and of design in the 1990s.

The introduction to this booklet mentions the healthy developments being generated by the younger generation and its questioning of old norms. Craftsmen experimenting with materials, techniques, function, line, colour and surface texture often create developments which are taken up by designers and manufacturers. In this way the basic research carried out by innovative artisans is a precondition for the vitality of Sweden's design in general.

SWEDISH GLASS AND METTLESOME METALS

In the world of the crafts, Swedish glass is the best known material at international level, and development work is being done at large glassworks like Orrefors and Kosta Boda as well as in the studios of individual craftsmen. At Orrefors, for instance, Per B. Sundberg has been using the new Fabula technique – a kind of transfer method transposed to glass from the manufacture of porcelain – to create encapsulated fantasy worlds. Glass production in small Swedish studio workshops is vigorous, and contributes to the development of the field, even though its practitioners find it more difficult to get a viewing due to the dominance of the big glassworks. Examples of pioneers here are Ulla Forsell, Gunilla Kihlgren, Mårten Medbo and Ditte Johansson.

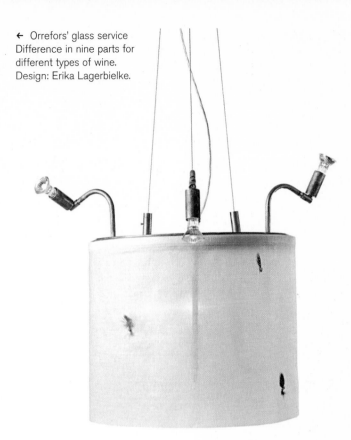

← Orrefors' glass service Difference in nine parts for different types of wine. Design: Erika Lagerbielke.

↑ The inimitable Jonas Bohlin's lamp, Circus.

↓ Glass artist Ulla Forsell has a rare gift for capturing Sweden's meadows in bloom.

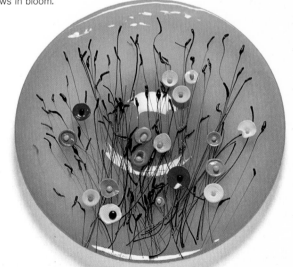

↑ Hanna Ljungström questions the shapes and expressions of the artisan tradition.

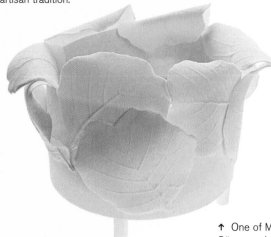

↑ One of Mia E. Göransson's bonbon-nières.

↓ Olle Brozén is the most recent designer to be employed by Kosta Boda.

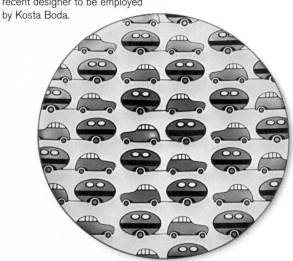

With some 15 glassworks, the Kingdom of Crystal (Glasriket) in Småland in southern Sweden is one of the country's favourite tourist attractions, with the Glass Museum in Växjö as its central hub. Furthermore, every three years international glass-collectors book a ticket to the Global Glass Art exhibition in Borgholm in Öland where the world's finest glass artists exhibit their work.

Swedish metalwork, principally in the form of jewellery, is gaining ground, as witness the Nordic jewellery triennial which was held for the second time in 2002. Here many big issues were captured in small objets d'art – as in the brooches of Ulrika Swärd which encapsulate her commentary on the decline and fall of the Swedish "folkhem" ("Home of the People", an idyllic vision of socially engineered prosperity) welfare state. Other popularizers of Swedish metalwork are Contemporary Swedish Silver and Metallum in Stockholm and the Hnoss gallery in Gothenburg, which between them gather the elite of Swedish gold- and silversmiths, including Helena Sandström, Erik Tidäng, Petra Schou and Anders Ljungberg.

FULL-BLOODED CERAMICS AND TEXTILE STATUS

Swedish ceramics have their blood up and show enormous vital-ity and a number of gifted young artists are advancing boldly. An example is Eva Hild, who extends the limits of stoneware with her sensuous, organic shapes, while Backa Carin Ivarsdotter's auto-destructive sculptures have a magical quality, as do her ceramic tiles with their elongated tentacles. And then the myriad ways a Swede can interpret Swedish flora and fauna! Mia Göransson with her bonbonnières and wall mosaics ornamented with delicate buds, twigs and leaves, and Adrienne Riesley with her cow heads of lace, clay and iron, taking our thoughts back to an age when meadows were not sprayed with pestkillers and every child had patted a calf.

The status of textiles is rising as a joint forum for Swedish textile artists is being developed in a cooperative effort between the Textile Museum, the School of Textiles in Borås and the Röhsska Museum in Gothenburg. At the same time a number of individual Swedish textile artists are heading abroad, fascinated by artists like Pasi Välimaa. With his sensuously undulating chiffon fabrics and textile mosaics he is able to infuse beauty with content. Katrina Berglund opens up new possibilities for textiles with her knitted bowls in incandescent colours, as does Kajsa af Petersens with her filmy nets and delicate tangles.

FUTURISTIC PREDICTIONS

Predicting the fortunes of Swedish design would appear to be a relatively simple challenge, even though the field is very sensitive to economic ups and downs. Many of current strengths will develop further, so that design with a dual dimension combining democracy and humanity will remain a Swedish hallmark. Ergonomics and a caring attitude towards vulnerable groups in society will grow in importance, particularly with the coming old-age population explosion in the world, and these are spheres in which Swedes have both great commitment and a great deal of knowledge. Good design in public spaces, and in the working environment, will remain important facets of Swedish wellbeing.

Just as sure is the conviction that Swedish industry will become a more and more eager and aware purchaser of design services, and that Swedish well-trained and highly skilled designers will enhance their reputation as attractive workers and partners both at home and abroad. With knowledge, awareness, creativity and enthusiasm in abundant supply, this is a real possibility.

→ Bamboo King, Mats Theselius' most recent armchair for Källemo.

↓ Ulrica Hydman-Vallien.

GET IN TOUCH, READ AND LEARN MORE

www.scandinaviandesign.com
(contains links to several companies and designers)

www.svenskform.se

www.svid.se

Form the Design Magazine, (in Swedish and English) www.svenskform.se

Stockholm New, (in English) www.stockholmnew.com

The Swedish Architecture & Design Yearbook, Arvinius förlag (in English)
www.arvinius.se

Swedish Design by Denise Hagströmer/The Swedish Institute, (in English)
www.si.se

Swedish Design – the best of Swedish design today, by Susanne Helgeson
and Kent Nyberg/Prisma, (in English, the Swedish version is called *Svenska
Former*) www.bokus.com

Photos: Cover: Claesson Koivisto Rune. Page 1 top: Koenigsegg CC V8 S; design by David Crafoord/
Ergonomidesign, Joachim Nordwall, Fredrik Åsell and Christian von Koenigsegg. Swivel armchair and stool from
Swedese, design Joel Karlsson. Bottom: Jeans candlestick by Zandra Ahl. Slowfox for Orrefors by the doyen of
Swedish glass Ingegerd Råman.

PHOTOGRAPHERS:
COVER: JESSICA GOW/PRESSENS BILD. AUTHOR'S PORTRAIT: CATO LEIN. PAGE 1, CANDLESTICK: ANNA KLEBERG. 2 TOP, COVER PHOTO
OF CROWN PRINCESS VICTORIA: MIKAEL JANSSON. 5 TOP: ANNIKA EKBLOM. 6 BOTTOM: MICHAEL PERLMUTTER. 8 TOP: SHARIF SHAWKY.
9, RECLINING CHAIR RELAX: JONAS LINELL. 10, KNIFE AND SPOON: PEER ERIKSSON. 11 BOTTOM AND 34 BOTTOM: PELLE WAHLGREN.
15 BEATRICE LUNDBORG/PRESSENS BILD. 20 BOTTOM AND 26: FREDERIK LIEBERATH/CAMERA LINK. 22 FREDRIK PERSSON/PRESSENS
BILD. 23 BOTTOM: PELLE STRENGBOHM. 28 ANETTE NANTELL/PRESSENS BILD. 31 JONAS EKSTRÖMER/PRESSENS BILD. 33 TOP: LENNART
KALTEA, BOTTOM: ANDERS QVARNSTRÖM. 34, BONBONNIÈRE: SARA DANIELSSON. 35 BOTTOM: THOMAS PERSSON/PRESSENS BILD.